The Boundary Is You

How to create boundaries by loving yourself more

By

Chany G. Ro

Dedication

For Pinchus

My partner in all the preciousness of life. You welcome my evolution.

Table Of Contents

Chapter 1

Love and Acceptance

D o you hate yourself?

Whoa.

Hate may be a very strong word, especially for a person like you, who is successful, smarter than most, and eats their vegetables.

But also: your insides gnaw with self-doubt, and you rethink many of the things you once did, bringing up a cesspool of shame. Your relationships are lackluster, often painful, and highlight how alone and unsupported you really are. You smile and say yes to people, when what you really mean to say is, "Please go away and ask someone else." You watch other people do things which, had life turned out differently, you would have loved to do yourself. You don't trust people, not even those closest to you, especially after what they've done. You don't like yourself.

You may not relate to all of these specifics, but if you picked up this book, you want one thing: to feel good, even in your current relationships.

I'm Chany Rosengarten, and I want to gently hold you by the elbow as you walk toward loving yourself – creating safe, healthy boundaries inside of your relationships. Okay?

We are going to be learning boundaries, but we'll do it in a new way: a way that works.

Boundaries are often seen as the rules we set up with others. But can we be honest with each other here? Boundaries that focus on the other person don't work, nor do they help.

What you really need is to stop hating yourself. You want your relationships to stop hurting. You want the pain, loneliness, shame, overextending yourself to stop.

What you really need is to start caring for yourself. You want to stop being afraid of being yourself. You want to accept your choices. You want to be free to ask for what you need … and get it. You want to give yourself permission to live the life you've always pushed off.

What you really need to know is that the boundary is you. You have all the power to shift a relationship. You have the rights to your own life.

When you are done, you'll know why self-love is so important to your relationships, and you'll know just what to do to get there. You'll be able to look in the mirror and smile (without taking note of your too-large nose, waist or shoe size). You'll wake up feeling free. Best of all, you'll finally take action on behalf of yourself, creating the relationships you so richly deserve.

Welcome to the Club

People who don't like themselves make up at least 59 percent of us. And self-loathing leads to all kinds of things, none of them a deep appreciation for self, life and others, coupled with an inner peace and confidence.

The symptoms of self-hatred run the gamut. I'll list them here. Do me a favor – check off the ones that apply to you.

- Perfectionism
- Superiority. You are smarter, faster, stronger, more elegant or talented, and also better in a general way. This often comes with a self-satisfying sniff when in the presence of those who don't meet your standards.
- Serial seriousness, because the rest of humanity just doesn't get it, but you do. This world is a somber place. None of us get out alive.
- The need to prove yourself
- A brutal inner critic
- Putting yourself down in a cute, self-deprecating way
- Comparing yourself to others
- Self-sabotage where it's about to get good, and you get that feeling like, Nah. This doesn't feel

right. So you do something about it, and things feel right again.

- Avoiding positive action
- Not brushing your teeth, washing your laundry or other activities that make up the tedious part of life
- Lack of success
- Survivor's guilt, or why you can't enjoy yourself, citing children in Africa, grandparents in Auschwitz, and the fact that we are all in the top five percent if we are able to read this book.
- Addiction. Or just a really tight relationship with wine, beer, liquor, scotch, drugs of all kinds, including prescribed ones.
- Isolation
- An obsession with love, romance or sex
- A tendency to fight people, even when it is justified
- Self-harm
- Suicidal thoughts
- Abusive relationships
- Poor parenting
- Neglecting yourself and playing the martyr

- Victimization
- Rage. Anger, expressed with real passion.
- Depression
- Dissociation, where it's so painful to be you, you find ways to stop being you, if only in your own mind.
- Eating disorders
- Ruminating over interactions and wishing you could have a rerun, where you'd do it much better.
- Shame
- Unworthiness

If you've checked off one of these or more, you are not alone, and in fact you are part of the majority. Welcome to the club. We've been waiting for you here. All is not lost. In fact, the good times are just beginning. Because it's brave people like you, who are willing to raise your hand and say, "Yeah … that's me," who are the front runners in healing themselves and the world.

It takes brutal honesty to say, "I don't really like this person who is me."

Me. The successful author, the authoritative manager, the mother of three little ones who managed to offer my kids enrichment programs, the friend, the chef, me. I don't really like me all that much.

Once you admit that, you are halfway there. And this book will take you even further.

Think about this: If each of these symptoms has an underlying cause of not respecting ourselves, imagine what just a little bit of self-love could do. Self-love is the leading cause of:

- Successful, long term relationships
- Positive parenting and children who grow up with a good sense of self
- Healthy boundaries
- Positive attitudes
- The ability to deal with challenges
- Motivation for healthy habits
- Successful negotiation
- The ability to connect
- A sense of serenity
- Reduced stress and anxiety
- A boost in attractiveness

- Personal growth
- Self esteem

I think we are beginning to detect a pattern here. Self-love = good outcomes. Self-hatred = a slew of painful outcomes.

If you are in a relationship, but in that relationship you really don't like yourself all that much, guess what that relationship will look like?

No need to guess, right? This is your life.

My Journey to Self-Love

I didn't always know how to love myself. In fact, I didn't consider self-love to be important. It seemed superfluous and stupid, to be honest, because those people who did seem to love themselves did it at great peril. They weren't even that amazing, and they blithely ignored that fact, to their own detriment.

My self-critic was not only my closest confidant, but also my protector. Thanks to its watchful influence, I was constantly spared from saying anything foolish (we reviewed for hours after each encounter), doing anything that made me look bad, or living fully.

If my self-loathing would have been confined to my teenage years, I may have written it off as one of the costs of adolescent angst. Alas, not knowing how to love myself didn't simply resolve itself. It followed me into adulthood. It shadowed me on my job, sat in on my marriage, and ruled in my parenting. And even though self-hatred cast havoc wherever both of us went, my commitment to my inner critic was steadfast.

The only reason I came to love myself was because nothing was working, and I needed to heal my heart.

And so, marriage, job, money, parenting, sanity in shambles, I found the one common denominator in all of this: me. And when I found me, I noticed she was in handcuffs, hijacked by the hater who kept me believing I was inherently flawed and that I needed to prove my worth and value, if I were to live.

It started when I was in second grade.

I was expelled from school.

We lived in a very small village with one private school. My place was secure in that school, having nowhere else to go. Until my principal grabbed my arm with her chapped hands and spat out: "Go home to your mother and tell her what you did."

"What *did* I do?"

"Leave."

So I left, walking down the tree-lined street and into the kitchen. My mom wasn't very happy to see me. She had been perfectly content paying tuition to have me out from under her feet. She called the school. The school told her that I had laughed when the principal admonished the students for rowdy behavior.

My mother sided with the school, possibly because she was employed with them. "She is a very difficult child."

Thus began my confusion, and my career as the class clown and troubled student. In every subsequent year I was expelled again, and the cycle repeated itself.

Years later, having the compassion for the child I had been in second grade, I understood that laughing when my principal was at the height of her speech to the class was my own way of releasing tension and fear from my body. But that was twenty years in the future.

For now, that little girl took on the identity she had been given. I was difficult. Rowdy. Unbearable. Insolent. And definitely undeserving of a place among my peers, though I didn't know why. Which was confusing. Was it my voice? Looks? What I said? Did? Didn't say? Did I smell bad?

One thing was clear. I wasn't deserving of love.

That a girl who was kicked out of school "for good" every single year could become a teacher in that same school was unimaginable. And yet there I was, freshly graduated from high school, and being offered not one, but three positions.

One was in the English department, seventh grade. One was an extracurricular enrichment program for second through fifth grades, offered by the same principal who had kicked me out that first time, but was now wildly enthusiastic about hiring me. And the third required travel, but was the best paying and most prestigious of the lot.

I wanted the travel one. But my mother discouraged me. She said she'd pull some strings to help me get the

11

seventh grade local job, because "it would fetch you a better marriage prospect."

I called back the two other women and thanked them for the offer. And I turned myself in for a year of harassment, shaming and criticism. The first day, dressed for success and nervously entering the staff room, my new employer told me, "You can't step foot in here wearing this." I was wearing my favorite camel skirt and a blouse imported from Germany. The next day, she walked me into class, stood at the door while I taught for the first time, and then called me out, criticizing my lack of confidence and my teaching style.

Slowly, whatever sense of self I had left siphoned off. Weight I had always wished to shed fell away. My ability to think and remember was compromised. I couldn't sleep. And I suffered from acute anxiety.

But it was all good, because – I got engaged.

This is how I started my adult life. In an atmosphere of zero self-respect, where being myself was not good enough, where I was deserving of love only if I'd be the person I was not, I started my own family.

I felt angry, but not having context on why being valued was important, I didn't know why I was angry. I felt confused, overwhelmed, unloved. That toxic cocktail of emotions didn't have enough room in one body. Some of it was poured onto my new husband, who hadn't even been involved in all the drama and pain leading up to our marriage. Some of it was placed in the jurisdiction of my tiny, newborn child, born pure and innocent, but in the shadow of my pain. Most of it I internalized as a hard ball of self-hatred, becoming depressed, desperate and despairing of ever feeling whole again.

To give you a summary of everything that followed in the next ten years: it didn't go well.

I made sure it looked good. I built a career that I could finally hold as a trophy and say, "See, I am worth something." I parented my kids on both ends of the pole of liberal and totalitarian values. And I moved to another continent. But through it all, I woke up every day hating myself, and I went to sleep with proof that the hatred was well grounded.

I lost most of my joy. I ground through day after day, working hard to prove that I was worthwhile and, if not lovable, then at least tolerable, all the while seeking for it to end in the oblivion of sleep. I relied on chocolate and other sweets to numb my feelings, which worked some of the time. I sought relationships in which I felt either superior or victimized, and I fed off gossip, just to live vicariously through the trials of others.

But one day, the pain was so strong that I couldn't escape it. My husband and I fell out of the hellish dance of cycling through hating and shaming, apologizing and forgiving, making up and trying, only to repeat when the relationship got too close for comfort. My obsession with success didn't work anymore because I had attained a measure of it, and it offered no reprieve. I finally faced myself in the mirror, and saw a person I deeply disliked living with.

I knew something had to shift. And it did.

I reached through the dark smog for the chance of something better. I went from hating to accepting and loving myself. I found a better way.

And I want you to do the same.

I want you to love yourself. I can't say it more plainly. I want you to love yourself.

The bravest action you will ever take is to accept yourself, just as you are. I know you can do it, because I did it, and I will walk you through this, step by step. Together, this will be doable. It will also be the most courageous thing you have ever asked of yourself.

But you must do this.

Don't do it for yourself, you loathsome, despicable thing. Just kidding. Yes, do it for yourself. But also do it so your relationships will start working. Do it for your children. Your sisters. Your friends. Do it for anyone on the planet who, by seeing you shine, will know it is possible.

When we don't accept parts of ourselves, we have interactions where we hoist the unacceptable parts of ourselves onto others. We wait for others to confirm how pain-worthy we are, and generously, they comply. We pass on all our unfinished business to our children. Our employees, colleagues and clients are at the receiving end of our internal wrath. In our intimate relationships, we can only be as intimate as the places we have loved. All else is walls.

The world is waiting for you to be in your fullness. The entire population needs you to be your best self. The people who are most intimately affected by you need you to love yourself.

I made a pact with myself that if I ever got out from under the abuse that was my daily self-talk and that I allowed to be mirrored back to me, I would teach others to do the same. I'll teach you how to do it, and you will do it.

So do we have a deal?

Agreed. We have a deal. Let's go.

Chapter 2

Boundaries

What are boundaries?

Boundary: a line or limit that marks where two things become different. When it comes to relationships, a boundary is the line that marks where you end and another person begins.

In its simplest form, having boundaries is knowing yourself. When you know who you are, you know where you begin, and where you end. You accept yourself. You love yourself. You can feel if you want something or not. You know when someone has gotten too close, or when you are chasing someone who is unavailable or backing away.

Why are boundaries important?

Well, let's talk about what happens when we don't have boundaries. Without the line, without knowing where we end and someone else begins, we bleed right into each other.

When I got married, I was happy to bleed right into my husband. If I had no self, I was happy to take on his self. The problems with this approach are many, as you can imagine. I deferred to him, until I felt stifled and trapped in a life that barely resembled mine. And while I wasn't living my life, I wasn't living his, either, because it's impossible, or at best burdensome, to try living through someone else.

But it was the only approach I knew, until I learned about boundaries. Once I learned who I was, I let him live for himself and me for myself, and connected from a place of wholeness.

Boundaries are knowing all of who you are, and seeing where you end. It's seeing any other person as a completely separate person. In every interaction, boundaries are the awareness of how you, in your fullness and limitations, are interacting with the other person's fullness and limitations. It's the awareness of where both of you start and end.

We need boundaries so that in all our relationships, we can stay with ourselves while also being present with the other person. Boundaries allow us to connect without getting lost in the connection. Boundaries give us a sense of safety, even in challenging interactions, but especially in loving ones. Boundaries are what allow us to connect deeply. Boundaries keep us safe.

Lack of boundaries leads to confusion. We have a lot of wisdom inside of us. But when we are disconnected from ourselves, we are distanced from our source of wisdom and we become paralyzed by indecision, doubt and confusion. We start taking on the other person's reality, which may be wise for them, but isn't ours. Going back to yourself will bring you back to your wisdom.

Living without boundaries is the cause of many of the pains that plague relationships, and even ourselves.

Abuse is an outcome of a lack of boundaries. Victims can heal by learning boundaries, too. If you've been in a relationship that feels tricky, and you try to navigate its pitfalls, going back to loving yourself will be your companion so you can steer your way through.

When we establish boundaries, we are surveying the lay of the land of who we are, and recognize just how far we are willing to go. We decide who we are in any given relationship. Whether it is in business, romance, family or friendships, we remain attuned to who we are and maintain that core existence.

Boundaries are who you are. You don't have to make boundaries. You don't need to erect fences in order to be safe. You don't need to cut off loved ones.

But you do need to know yourself, and love yourself enough to advocate for yourself when others are stepping all over you. The better you know yourself, the more you are aware of when something or someone crosses the line of how far you are willing to go. You know what doesn't resonate. If you know your limitations, you know how far you are willing to go, and if you have gone too far. You are willing to put yourself first.

You Already Have Boundaries

If a boundary is the line that marks where you end and another person begins, don't you already have those lines?

Let's think about someone who crossed all the lines. Have you ever come in contact with someone like that? Total disregard toward the cues you were sending, stepping all over your feelings, ignoring your requests, mocking you for your needs.

If you're anything like me, when the person took that first step to cross a clear line, you were so shocked, you may have stayed silent, just observed, perhaps allowed the invasion to happen.

You hated yourself for it, but you semi-blamed yourself, and you were also confused. It may have continued, with you feeling uneasy about the relationship. Sometimes boundaries get crossed so subtly, over such a long time, that as the trespasser gets closer to the core, you barely register what is happening. You think something is wrong with you. You agree with the boundary crosser.

But what happened when this boundary crosser crossed one line too many?

You may have cried. You may have momentarily felt enraged. You may have felt yourself going numb, dissociating, your consciousness leaving your body. You may have felt nauseated or disgusted.

That was you upholding your boundaries.

We don't always uphold all of our boundaries. It can be confusing to know where we start and the other person ends. Seasoned boundary crossers are skilled at turning their issues into your issue, and that makes it even more confusing. But when you know, you know. When someone has cut too close to the chase, you know. You know you've been crossed.

The steps you took when that happened may have seemed weak and disempowered. But they were steps nonetheless.

That was you standing up for your boundaries.

My sister knew how to establish her boundaries. When she didn't want something, she had this way of saying no. It was just one word: no. That's all she did. But when she said it, she meant it.

There was the time we were both helping my aunt, who ran a seasonal sewing business, right before the holiday. The work was piled up all over the house. There was work everywhere. And at one point my sister said, "I'm done for the day."

That was it. My aunt asked her if she had any extra time. "No."

And that was that. She went downstairs, slipped on her coat, and left.

What about me? I saw the work, and I saw that if I pushed myself, the work would get done. So I worked until the kink in my left shoulder throbbed with pain. I worked until long after my bedtime. I worked and worked.

I liked working. I loved my aunt, still do, and I was willing to put my own comfort on the side for that love.

I didn't know that I could have that love without putting my own life aside. I didn't know that love was fun and it was free.

I couldn't forgive myself for not saying no. Why couldn't I do what my sister did, where the smallest word was an indisputable fact? Where was I on my own behalf when I took a teaching job that would rob me of my dignity? Where was that little no when I needed it? Where was my no when my parents ran after a marriage prospect in an exchange that felt like they were selling me off to the lowest bidder?

I wanted my sister's no.

But I realized this: even though I didn't know how to make boundaries because I didn't know how to honor the boundary I was, there were boundaries there. There were tears. There was anger. There was my left shoulder, always telling me when enough had been enough. There were natural boundaries. And as soon as I became willing to honor them, those boundaries were there for me.

Natural Boundaries

The natural world desires to be more of itself. It wants to spread far and wide and propagate. Yet if any one element crosses the lines and monopolizes the world, the delicate equilibrium in the ecosystem loses its vital balance. For the world to maintain its existence, it must have the essential element of natural boundaries.

Take the ocean. The ocean wants to cover all of the earth. Every moment of every day, the ocean throws itself against the sand, pounding the seashore with desperate waves. The land stands firm: "Until here you go, and no further." And the waves retreat, only to try again.

The body, too, has boundaries. The skin is a boundary for microscopic invaders that want to overtake, weaken and kill the body. Millions of bacteria attempt to reproduce on every surface, so more of itself will exist. Every day we have multiple protections, from skin to saliva to mucus to tears, that wash it all away and keep our bodies safe for ourselves.

The skin has boundaries, too. We clothe the body as a boundary that lets others know that our bodies are not accessible. We clothe ourselves to convey a message of who we are. We dress up or down to indicate our identity.

Access to ourselves, even fully clothed, is also limited. We have boundaries around our space. Nobody can come closer than our personal space without clearly violating a boundary. Our home is our own, and only those who are invited may enter. We don't always allow our guests access to our bedrooms, to our closets or to our home office. We allow with discretion.

Our office, or personal desk, is ours. Our car is ours. We may decide to share them, but we know who holds ownership over these things. Those are our boundaries. And even when we do open up a boundary and welcome someone in, we do so at the level we are comfortable with, to the people we are safe with.

Can you see that you already have so many boundaries naturally in place?

Within your psyche, too, you have boundaries.

Your soul, or your life force, is not limited. It wants to be all of itself. It is intrinsically unlimited and boundless. Yet without the limitations of a body, your soul cannot find expression in the real world. The body is a container for the soul. It is the boundary. The body limits, but also gives expression to the soul. The body is bound to time, space and a whole bunch of traumas and messages it has picked up on the way. The soul is not. But the soul works within the boundary of the body.

You can have boundaries on your time. You don't have to give it all away. Time has inherent boundaries, such as night and day, months and years. Life itself doesn't go on forever, but is finite and very clear cut. We often give away our time to people or missions that don't interest us, leaving little of our time to enjoy experiences that enrich us. Since your time is limited, it's up to you to work with your natural time boundary and use your time well.

Our brains have boundaries too. Although the world is full of stimuli, we filter out irrelevant sounds and sights. Our brain is wired to pick up what it's been primed to see. You choose where to focus. The book that everyone is reading is not necessarily the book I'm reading, if it doesn't talk to exactly what I need right now. The guru everyone is seeing is also only mine if he is teaching the ideas that matter to me. All else is noise, and you can disregard it at any time.

You may have allowed someone to cross some boundaries, but remember, *you* are a boundary. Your body is a boundary. Your home is a boundary. Your room is a boundary. You're not a lost cause when it comes to boundaries.

In fact, recognizing what you already have is the first level of boundaries. I am Chany. I have ten fingers and ten toes. This is where I live. I am not my neighbors. I am not my sister. I am not experiencing my sister's struggle. I know where I end, but most important, I know what and who I am. I am a human being, a natural at boundaries. I am not a loser at boundaries.

When you come back to yourself and you leave all the others outside of you, where they firmly belong, that's you experiencing intimacy with yourself. You're looking at yourself, and you're finally meeting yourself, minus all the noise. You start noticing how completely awesome you are.

Boundaries and Self-Love

Why do we need to love ourselves in order to have real, insurmountable boundaries?

Boundaries are challenging because we actually love the people we need to make boundaries with. These are our closest relationships. We love them and we want the connection. We are willing to make sacrifices because of our love.

But when our boundaries disappear, those sacrifices are too costly. They cost us ourselves.

There has to be a better way to make boundaries than to shut them out.

And there is.

As you get in touch with yourself, you know what you need. You start trusting that what you need is important. You start believing that getting what you desire is possible. You gain confidence in your ability to ask. Part of you once believed that your sanity, peace, happiness and wellbeing was in the hands of another person. You needed that individual to be the person who could give you what you needed.

Not anymore. You have yourself now.

I remember reading a book about assertiveness. The knot in my stomach was pretty assertive. Me, on the other hand? Not so much.

The book had been handed to me by my employer. I was working at that first year teaching job.

And I was failing.

I stood in front of the classroom, afraid of the twenty-five seventh graders who looked up at me from their desks, half expectantly, half challenging. I stammered. I forgot what I was going to say, instead looking around the classroom and at the large window in the door where the principal stood, not hiding her disappointment as she observed me stumbling through the lesson.

One day, a student of mine disrupted the class. I would have ignored it like I did all the others, not having the tools to deal with her. But the principal was there, perched at her observation window, and she gave me exact instructions. Send the girl out to wait. Finish teaching. Give her a talking to. If I couldn't do that, then I really couldn't continue teaching in the school. She even told me what to tell this student, word for word.

But as I stood face to face with the young girl, my own panic, failure and shame overwhelmed me. I didn't know what to say. I tried remembering what my principal had instructed, but I drew a blank. The girl backed into a corner. I felt sorry for both of us.

And that's how I was given the book on assertiveness, and read its meaningless words again and again, trying to make sense of it. I didn't learn assertiveness that day. Instead, I finished the school year four sizes smaller than I had started, and slunk out of there to collect the pieces of myself and glue them back together.

You can't be assertive when you have nothing to assert.

You can't have boundaries when you don't know who you are.

You can't experience dignity when your insides are coiled up in shame.

You can't have others respect you when you love them more than you like yourself.

The LAND method you are about to learn is about loving yourself into *becoming* the boundary. *You* are the boundary. You can set boundaries, assert boundaries and fight for your boundaries, but if *you* are not the boundary, all that is useless. Trust me, I've tried it all.

What this book will give you is the gift of knowing who you are, loving who you are through this brave process of becoming more yourself. You are going to go from hating yourself to caring for yourself, even within the context of your current relationships. You will go from ignoring your needs, from, "Nah, I'm good" (I'm really starved for this thing, and I've worked all my life for it and it hurts to see it being given away to someone else who doesn't deserve it, but hey, I'm cool), to asking for your needs and getting them. You are going to go from relationships that don't work because you don't think you deserve any better, to relationships that honor you.

The more you return to your essential self, the closer you are to your natural boundaries and the harder it is to violate them again. You are an adult now. You don't have all the power – you will still run into challenging situations – but you have wisdom. And you have the ability to take yourself back to love. You have the ability to make boundaries based on love.

Our souls are pure love. They are limitless and they are expansive. But as soon as we squeeze into a body and take on physicality, we also sign up for limitations. All of us live in a limited body, born to limited parents, transition from unlimited to limited, from soul to body, from free to confined. It's part of the human condition.

Even though you were born with boundaries clearly protecting your soul, you may have lost them as a child. But you are here now, and you are ready. It's time to return back to who you are. It's time to return to love.

If boundaries are hard for you, know this: it's normal for boundaries to be hard. But if you are filled with such self-respect that you mean what you say, then you have words to protect you. If you are a carrier of self-care, your dignity is your guide. You intuitively know how to handle situations that used to take you out. You know, because you are led by one guiding principle: I am worthy.

The LAND Method

The LAND method is based on your natural self, so you don't have to fight against yourself. When we fight against ourselves, we always lose: if we win, we've lost, and if we've lost, we've lost. It's us we are fighting against, and the stakes are always against us. Instead, the LAND method takes you back to your natural boundaries.

I formulated this method when I was sitting on the beach, considering how challenging it is to establish boundaries when we live with difficult people. The waves kept crashing up onto the land at the seashore, and I thought, LAND! That's it.

That's our process.

Land simply is. It stands there, inert, all the miniscule grains of it, just sitting there. It's dealing with a force so vehement and so powerful, so hungry and so fierce.

The land is the boundary to a force that continues to saturate it. And yet it just stands there.

In being itself, the land tells the ocean: be all you can be. Throw yourself on me. Attempt to saturate me. Attempt to wash me into your hunger. No matter what you throw at me … I'll just be here.

That's the power of the land. The land on the beach is the natural boundary for the ocean. On its surface, civilization grows. People, livestock, trees, food sources all flourish. In its wisdom, the land allows in as much water as it needs for itself, and sends the rest back, up in the clouds, into the ocean.

Being is a boundary. Being *you* can be *your* boundary. Accepting you, loving you, being all of you is a powerful boundary. Boundaries are a natural part of you, and once you lean into it, you'll find your boundaries quite natural to establish.

The LAND method is a simple, four step process. When you are in a situation where you are interacting with another person and you are feeling uncomfortable, you can check in with the four steps of

35

the LAND method to make sure that your boundaries are okay.

The four steps of the LAND method are:

1. Love
2. Authority
3. Negotiation
4. Direction

Love: How can you love and accept yourself in this situation?

Authority: What is the power *you* have within this situation? Hint: it's not the other person. You don't have power over another human being. Your *own* power is unlimited.

Negotiation: How can you communicate honestly, in a way that gets your needs met?

Direction: Where are you headed in your life? How would you ideally like your life to be?

You'll follow the four steps to learn and practice loving yourself. And boundaries will become something you do as naturally as breathing, or walking, or living.

Your boundary is *you*. Your boundary just *is*. It's not negotiable.

Chapter 3

The First Step –
Love Yourself.

Self-love is loving the self that is you. That ugly, angry, sweaty self that is you. That lonely, too busy, messy desk self that is you.

The first thing to do when you need to find your boundaries is go heavy on the love you have for yourself. Otherwise you are doomed to need the love of the other person, to the point where separating who you are and who they are is impossible.

So let's talk about love. Let's talk about you.

Why would we talk about you when we talk about love?

Because you *are* love. Underneath all the layers, the things you've done and the things you didn't do, the things you tried doing but failed at and the things other people did that messed with you, under it all is love.

We'll be using the words 'you' and 'love' interchangeably, because they are synonymous.

While we often equate love with doing, achieving, proving, receiving or giving, real love just *is*. Breathe in, breathe out, that's you. You're not what you do, although you may have spent a lifetime believing it and trying to achieve it.

Here is how you can know this for certain: if you stop breathing for three minutes, that's it. You've ceased to exist, at least in this life form.

If you stop practicing law or medicine, you don't cease to exist. You may become depressed or you may reinvent yourself, but you won't cease to exist. If you stop talking to your spouse, you won't cease to exist. If you stop being cool, you won't cease to exist. If you lose a vital part of yourself, like your ability to work out, iron shirts and pack lunches – or the ability to calm down the fighting or alcoholism between your parents – you still won't cease to exist. Things may go bonkers for a while, but life will eventually figure itself out and continue. Life has this odd way of keeping on going.

The only way you will cease to exist is if you stop doing the only thing that is really, essentially, unforgettably you: if you stop breathing.

Your essence is your breath. Your essence is you existing. Being in the moment. Being alive. Being in this world, zero strings attached.

That state of being is love.

Often, when we seek to rectify a situation or relationship, we start from a place of business. "What can I do to fix this?" we ask. We try to fix the other, or if we're smart about how things work in the real world and recognize that we are simply incapable of fixing another, we turn to fixing ourselves.

The only way you can ever hope to change is if you give up on the change and just embrace yourself. You are good enough. If you are telling yourself, "Self-love has to wait until I'm done with self-renovation," you may spend years in a loop working on yourself. Working on yourself is convenient. It keeps you so busy fixing problems that you never have to actually resolve the issue. Loving yourself, even with all the reasons you believe you are unlovable, creates real space for empowered change.

We All Deserve Self-Love

You may feel anything other than love. You may feel guilty and wrong, as if most of you is polluted with your deeds. You may feel scared. You may feel undeserving. You walk around shying away from being seen. You work really hard to maintain your impossible standards and way of life to attain superiority. You may just feel exhausted. Love is the farthest thing from your mind.

When I was feeding myself my daily dose of judgement and self-hatred, I thought that the only way to experience love is to get love. I wasn't really lovable, but if my husband would show me a gesture of love, or he'd be in a good mood, or he'd notice my effort, then at least I had a crumb of self-worth to hold onto. This was a precarious situation, perched as I was in the hands of someone who was human himself, and thus loaded with his own shame messages.

Perhaps you can get love from a partner, or parent, or family member or friend who wants to love you. Perhaps you have to work for it. You may have to be a specific type or achieve certain measures of success to be loved by that person. You are willing to do anything, even if the price for that love is high and exhausting, because someone's got to love you. Perhaps you are chasing love that keeps slipping away. You see it from afar but you never really feel good, and when it is in your grasp, you push it away. You are proficient at repelling love or even compliments.

Let's talk about how to accept yourself. All of yourself. Even the parts of you that you believe deserve to die, if you could selectively assassinate them.

Why is this important? Why waste energy on accepting who we are, instead of seeking to transform it so we don't need to live with this?

I used to think it was essential to focus on change, not acceptance. Especially for the really important things. I could accept that I had a really bad memory. But I couldn't accept my poor parenting, which was riddled with bursts of rage. How could I accept something that, with each passing day it remained unchanged, radically affected my children's wellbeing?

I hated myself as a mom.

For years, rather than accepting the unthinkable – that I was a mom who tried her best and was simply imperfectly human – I believed in impossible standards that proved I was failing miserably. So I tried to change it. I attacked myself, telling myself that I had failed my children. I read all these magazines that said that the first three months, first year, three years, six years of a child's life are the ones that shape all the rest of his days, and I grieved for my boys, whose mother had been in a postpartum haze for all of that time. I took parenting classes with copious instructions that, in the blur of actual life, were completely untenable.

When I was consumed with baby care around the clock, my marriage tanked. I was overwhelmed just trying to get by. In retrospect, I was suffering from postpartum anxiety and depression. I felt like an absolute mess and totally alone.

And then my husband blamed me for poor parenting. I had never felt more burdened and resentful.

It took me years to recover my sense of normalcy and develop a relationship with the boys, all while feeding daily dinner and washing the laundry of two very small, very dirty kids.

But the boys were seven and eight now. And I was doing okay in my job and even picking up the pieces in my marriage. And yet I still hated myself as a mom. I wished I was more loving, patient and connected to them. I couldn't forgive myself for raising my boys in a dysfunctional home. Not only was it dysfunctional, but the dysfunction was me. I was so ill equipped to raise them.

I knew, through my work in therapy, that a lot of what we experience in adulthood is unresolved childhood trauma. And the amount of trauma I had passed onto these two was so unforgivable, I could barely look them in the eye.

But look them in the eye I did, because these children wanted me to watch their plays – long, drawn out, meandering dramas. I strained to follow but lost interest very early in scene one. These kids wanted to talk. They wanted, they wanted, they wanted … and it made me ache.

It was hard to access love in all this pain.

I was cleaning my boys' bedroom, which did not have the nautical theme I had always associated with good families, but instead was more of a dorm room … function meets boys. I was also crying, because my son had gotten so wild, he hurt his sister, and I raged at him …

My family seemed so far away from the descriptions given by parenting experts in the calm environment of their offices, while their children were safely in school.

That day I heard about boundaries. Not about making boundaries – I had tried that so many times. I heard about boundaries being who I was, and where I ended. I heard that I was separate from my children. That my children didn't start and end inside my bruised heart.

It was a radical thought, because I was so clearly their mother, so clearly the giver of all their childhood traumas, so clearly responsible for the insecure attachment they had experienced due to my preoccupation with myself and my troubles. I was so clearly responsible for all this dysfunction.

But I heard it nonetheless.

I was I. I was who I was.

And they were they. They were who they were.

I saw it so clearly now. My limitations. I was the type of girl who could dream in color, create and talk, but I wasn't a playdough master, linen changer or even child communicator. Inside the line of my limitations were all my strengths. But I wasn't a preschool teacher, try as I might, try as I did.

46

In this new light, I saw something else. Despite the fact that I was completely handicapped when it came to little children, I still showed up every single day. I had given them dinner. I had wiped my face after grieving my losses and listened to them babble on. It may have been with only half an ear, but I had listened. I was not cut out for this, yet I had done it.

"You have so much love for your children," my friend reflected to me once. "You are such a mama bear."

Me? I walked around with guilt, hatred and self-loathing every time I so much as came near my children, because all I could see was the damage I had done. My friend pointed out that the level of self-flagellation I had as a mom, and the level of rage I had toward myself, was indicative of how much I loved my children. Had I loved less, I would have been less fazed.

That had to be love. Nothing else would have propelled a girl like me to spend large amounts of time and energy on these little ones.

My friend gave me a prayer. "May you become the mother you already are."

I pass that on to you. May you be that which you already are. Amen.

The day I embraced my limitations was the day my heart exploded with love. I wasn't the loving mom that I had imagined moms to be. I was just myself. I recognized that the cookie baking together with little hands was a direct and free-flowing expression of the love I had to give. And so were the boys' bookshelves. And the stories I told them.

And if I could not listen to another drama, that was okay. That was what they had each other for – a willing audience.

Once I forgave myself for everything I had not given them, I was finally able to give them what I could. It still didn't measure up in my mind's eye to the imaginative mom ideal I had before I knew what having children entailed. But I could completely disregard the things I wasn't, because I knew who I was.

My limitations had set me free.

I was sitting on the sidelines of the Crayola factory, deeply engrossed in working on my tablet, when I looked up and saw my boys giggling, running between the activities and glowing with gladness. And it came to me in my freedom and total comfort with not involving myself with the exhibits, as some other parents were doing: my children had their boundaries, too. Their lives were not victimized by who I was. They were full human beings, as young as they were. They would figure out their lives. They would be okay. They would have limitations, perhaps a direct result of their childhood, but that was who they were, too.

At least one thing wouldn't be theirs to carry anymore. I had removed the burden of guilt and imperfection that I had previously thrust on them, a shadow of myself. I was okay. They were okay. We could all be ourselves.

Individuality and Conformity

I used to walk around thinking that I was crazy or weird. In my mind, there was one way to be: the way the majority of the people were.

I grew up in a small town, an insular community. Most of the people there adhered to the same way of life. There was a great sense of community, and I knew every single person on the grocery line, as well as what their foyers looked like on the inside. But it also made me doubt myself every time I came across something inside me that didn't fit in.

Most of us commune with people who have similar interests, beliefs or political persuasions. We can sense an outsider from miles away and will him to either conform or leave, lest he disrupts the status quo. Even as we protect our communal ways, we also defend our individuality. It's a difficult balance. Navigating the tightrope between individuality and community as a young child left me feeling less than. It gave me permission to hide who I was, and to feel shame.

Brene Brown writes in *The Gift of Imperfection*, "Fitting in is about assessing a situation and becoming who you need to be accepted. Belonging, on the other hand, doesn't require us to change who we are." It takes women well into their fifth decade to start accepting themselves, studies say. By that time, they have already raised a generation of mini self-haters who diligently follow in their footsteps. Some blame this on the media, who monger self-hatred in very specific and cruel forms while promoting the solution in the form of purchasable goods, which will finally allow you to be cool, pretty, flawless, or young again, as long as you are in possession of said item.

But the media is not entirely at fault.

We are born with both boundaries and dependencies. Your soul was born in its own sack of skin, bones and sinews. Before birth, when your life was fused with your mother's life and completely dependent on her wellbeing, she still had no awareness of your awareness. She could not think your thoughts, and she could not feel your feelings. Your experiences were your own. Yet if pregnant mom stopped breathing, you were dead.

As humans, we are dependent on other humans throughout our lives. We start off needing constant care: feeding, diapering, even our burping needs are supported. We need to be touched and held and spoken to in order to develop fully. We are completely in need of connection. Unlike other species who are born and stand on their feet within hours, often needing to escape their parents for their own safety, humans are wired for connection.

But that connection is not always available, and it's not always free.

We come into the world as vulnerable human beings, born to vulnerable human beings. We absorb what we have been given, not all of which is life affirming. Even in the most loving of homes, and especially in homes where there was dysfunction, fear, abuse, addiction, neglect or trauma, children pick up messages which they understand to mean, "You are unlovable."

So it remains, until someone decides to break the cycle.

Breaking the Cycle

When I got married to my husband, intimacy evaded me. It was the one thing I craved most, that deep connection in which I'd see and share, know and be known.

I *couldn't*.

To me, my husband represented shame. I could barely look him in the eye. Try connecting that way!

When we had met, my parents, having not cleaned out the shame they themselves carried, said to me, "Look, Chany. Nobody wants you. He is the only good boy who is willing to meet you. You must make a good impression."

Of course this wasn't true. Their perception of what constituted a "good boy" was limited to about 1.5 males between the ages of 18 and 18 plus 2 months, with very specific qualities, down to the style of shoes the young man chose to wear.

But the message stuck. It resonated with my already disenfranchised sense of self, and I bought into it. Instead of seeing a man who had a desire to commit to me and share a life together, I saw him as the last man on earth who, out of benevolence to the human race, was willing to procreate with me.

Naturally, connection failed.

The people were there. The ingredients were there. I was being called to it; it was right in front of me. Yet I couldn't.

If you have a desire, I'm going to guess that everything you need to fulfill that desire is closer than you think. It's probably right inside of you. That's why you're being called to it so strongly: it is calling you. What is in your way?

Today, married to the same guy, same children – though we've been blessed with two girls as additional gifts – I enjoy intimacy and love. I am supported and honored.

How did I get there? It took accepting everything that was between me and myself, so I could live with myself, and only then with him.

Deep as I was in my shame back then, I felt like I needed to hide every part of me that wasn't exactly like everyone else. I had to be as normal and non-weird as possible. I had to push parts of me down the cellar stairs so I could be accepted.

If I allowed myself a relationship with my husband at all, it was only with half of me, the parts of me that I trusted he deemed acceptable. And yet I wanted connection. It was only when I allowed myself to connect with *all* of who I was that I was able to connect with him.

How to Start Loving Yourself

Step 1 - Stop the Negativity

We don't have to go searching for love, just as the ocean does not go in search of water. It *is* water. You *are* love.

Instead, let's talk about all the things that drain love out of you, that divert this rich, natural resource out of your life. We want to reclaim it. If necessary, we will go to war to reclaim it. (Relax, it's not necessary, you can lay your arms down. May peace be with you.)

Let's get on with the task of removing the blockages that keep this love from you.

The first blockages are all the things you tell yourself about yourself. Non-complimentary things. Real things. Memories of every failure and shameful event that ever happened since you were in seventh grade.

You have experienced pain in your life. This is a fact.

You are not your own version of perfect. Even the people who have mastered the level of perfection that you desire in a certain area don't feel perfect, because perfect doesn't exist and is the most punishing of all human aspirations. You're not perfect, and you know it.

You're not even that good. You know the darkness that lies in your heart, the things you are capable of, the thoughts you've thought, the deeds you've done.

You may have made some pretty lousy choices. There is so much of you not to like, it's as if you are the most unlovable person on earth. Right?

How do I know this? Do you think I don't think these thoughts? I do. I've hated myself more than I've hated my enemies.

The human is inherently flawed. None of us come with perfectly symmetrical features, and none of us come without our own little package of dark emotions, such as jealousy, rage, hate and despair.

The human body is limited. The body is the boundary to your unlimited soul, and by its very nature will have cellulite and an accent and a tendency to burp.

Loving yourself means looking squarely and honestly into yourself and saying, even though I've hurt my sister, even though I let a friend abuse me and didn't clean the cobwebs in my dining room for two years, as well as ten million other things I wish I hadn't done or that hadn't been done to me, I still completely and totally accept all of me.

All. Of. Me.

Say it to yourself: Even though I did this (name the unforgivable, horrible, despicable act), I still completely and totally accept all of me.

Step 2 - Stop the Expectations

Perfection is conditional acceptance. I can't accept myself if I failed. I can't love myself if I still have ten extra pounds that I carry around like pot handles, and euphemistically call them love handles. I can't be loved if I have a temper. I don't deserve to live if I've done something bad like oversharing to the wrong person, so now, let a hole swallow me up. And my project that I've invested days, months, years into shouldn't see the light of day, because it got criticized.

Don't buy into the myth that the only way you are allowed to exist or thrive is if you meet up with all the expectations in your mind. Your mind always has a more upgraded picture than reality because it's not reality based, and in a millisecond can be airbrushed, repainted, broken and recreated, while reality is time bound and reality bound and thus limited.

We will never match up with our ideals.

Even if you reach the nearly impossible ideals you have in your head, this gives your mind permission to dream of even bigger realities, because in proving that the impossible was made possible, your expectations expand. Now there is a new level, an additional rung in the never ending ladder that extends all the way up into infinity.

We believe there are certain conditions that make us deserving of love. Those conditions are ever changing. Even when we meet them, and we do allow ourselves to be loved, it doesn't fill us. The love feels conditional because that's not real love. It's reward. We can feel it, and we still stay hungry. In response, we create another challenge, the next level, another excuse of why we can't be loved right now. And we keep working on the next level of challenge, laboring for the right to exist.

Please. Stop now.

You will never get there. You will never be loved for your accolades, because quite frankly, nobody cares. And those people who do or did care about you reaching certain milestones only did that because *they* didn't know how to love. They had never been unconditionally loved themselves, so they used all those conditions as distractions, the same way you do. When my child will achieve grades, make the team, win the game, get into the big leagues, make his own money, open his own company, sell his own company, sell multiple companies, go live in Maui, buy an island off Maui …

All these conditions keep that one thing, that scary, vulnerable thing called love, perpetually out of reach.

Love is close. It sees you. It accepts you. It desires you. It embraces you. And if that's an unfamiliar feeling, it can be bewildering, sending you scuttling back into the perfectionist race.

Perfectionism is the act of buying into conditional acceptance. It's normal to do that. All of us buy into it because we were raised knowing that if we did good, things would be good. We'd be loved and accepted.

Our peers, too, taught us this lesson early. Fit in, and you'll be okay. In my high school class, we had the race of religion. Be the most pious, serious, and inspired, but not too much, just the right amount to be "special" while also being "normal." With my neighbors, we had the shopping race. Buy the right brands, but don't overdo it to the point of pretentiousness, and don't ever risk looking cheap.

When I lived in Israel, where resources were less available, there was the cleanliness race. If you painted your walls with whitewash once a week, you were the winner. Once a day, and you were crazy.

Society dictates what the specifics of the race should be, but regardless of the details, this is always the message: be anything less than our narrow expectations, and you will be bullied, shunned, disdained and unseen into oblivion.

But you are an adult now. You live your own reality. You make the rules. And here's a new rule for you. You can mess up. Go down. Stay down. You can go as low as a human being can possibly go, which, for the record, is pretty low. And you are still love. Nothing can take that away.

And nothing can make it more, because what is eternal can't be multiplied. It simply is. You can embody this truth more. You can become connected to it in such a way that you lead your life based on this love. But the love itself is unflinching and unchangeable. It doesn't get scared if you become the President of the United States or if you land behind bars or if you do both.

You want to buy that house, do that nose job, get that promotion? Sure, go ahead. But not as a way to buy love. It's not fair to pay for the right to breathe air, and it's not possible to work and slave for love that is already you. You're a wonderful human being.

Step 3 – Stop Focusing on Change

The only way we can ever hope to change is if we give up on the change and just embrace ourselves. We are good enough just as we are.

Focusing on change prevents us from accepting ourselves, which is the bravest part of change and actually creates lasting effects. When something is painful, blame and action assuage the pain, if only for a moment, like a painkiller. We don't have to feel anything because we have a target for our hate: ourselves. Our self-loathing keeps us firmly where we are.

Self-love asks you to be. Be in the pain. It's okay that I was a complete idiot. Be okay. Be forgiving. Simply be.

And that is the bravest thing you can ever do.

Safety is the experience of being completely okay with being completely yourself. As soon as you respect all of who you are, you are safe, allowing healing to happen. Healing fills up the space you create when you don't pull against what is.

Healing happens for you. You don't heal a cut; nature takes care of that for you. If you tried to heal it yourself, rubbing it every hour, constantly opening up the bandage to check on its progress, you'd interfere with the natural healing process.

Growth happens for you. You don't prod a tree to grow. Nature does that for you. Every tree pushes constantly against the limitations of itself to become more.

You, too, are nature. You, too, naturally grow. All you have to do is provide the safety and space for that growth to happen.

You need a huge, gentle hug from yourself for where you are, the ability to look at yourself with compassion, and acknowledge to yourself that you've done enough. You've probably thrown every single thing in your power at this challenge. If there's anything more that you have the capacity of doing, you will do it. You're here for it.

But for today, where you are is here. Right here. Look around you. Here you are. You are at home in your life.

Where you are is okay. The pain you're feeling? The lack, that desperation to have it all line up, the desire to change, the relationship that drives you up a wall? You'll survive it. You don't need to do anything more and you don't need to push harder because the fact is, you've done enough.

The first step in getting anywhere is safety. Respect yourself, respect your process. Walk gently on sacred ground.

You may have been disrespected in your life. But you don't have to disrespect yourself. You may have received messages that your feelings or experiences are not valid. But don't tell yourself that what you are feeling right now must be forcibly changed. You may have felt that your perception of reality was denied. Lean into your reality.

You may have been told that who you are or what you desire to be has no importance. You may have chosen to listen to those messages and twist yourself around to deny them, until who you became was not who you knew yourself to be.

You can stop now. You are safe.

You can stop needing to be anything but what you are. Even if what you are is codependent and has low self-worth, that's okay. That was you taking the path you needed to take then.

You are okay. All of you, including your mistakes.

Most urges to change go something like this: "I will not be okay with who I am. I will keep pushing myself and prodding myself into a new state of reality." You urge yourself to lose the weight already, get out of the relationship already, release yourself from debt already.

If it would have been that simple, wouldn't you have done it already?

And now you're hating yourself for failing. In addition to the pain of hating yourself, there is the pain of failure. And if you're savvy enough to know that self-hatred isn't good for you, now you also hate yourself for hating yourself.

Let's do this: instead of fixing the problem, write it down.

And when you write it down, admit to yourself: there is nothing I can do about this.

You'll protest. There must be something. There is something! You haven't tried everything yet. There's still a lot more to try.

But just for today, write it this way: There is nothing I can do right now about (thing I despise about myself).

Write this too: I hate that thought, because living with (thing I despise about myself) makes all these other things happen. List the things that happen as a result.

When you're done writing it out, thank yourself for doing the brave work of acceptance.

You've been through a lot. And you still expect so much from yourself.

Be gentle. Act toward yourself as if you were your own loving mother. Hold your heart gently. Love yourself through your challenges.

Chapter 4

The Second Step – Autonomy

Autonomy is self-governance. Autonomy is knowing that even as we are in loving relationships with others, we are still ourselves. We can still take good care of ourselves. Our wellbeing is paramount.

A real relationship is this: two whole people, individually taking good care of themselves, and connecting from love and overflow. Autonomy is our ability to take good care of ourselves.

The Cycles of Depletion and Overflow

Have you ever done this? Give, give, and give some more to the people you love, until you are spent. You don't have time to take care of you. But you trust that *they* will take care of you.

Let's say you do this with your husband. You take care of his needs, cook his meals, drop off his shirts at the cleaners, host your in-laws. Your husband, in return, needs to take care of you. Often he is greeted by a resentful you, who wants him to get how hard it is and somehow intuitively know what you need. So he tries taking over your burden, exhausting himself. And you are holding his burden, exhausting yourself.

This is the cycle of depletion. Both people in a relationship are taking care of the other until they are spent. And as the stress grows, so does the need to take care of the other, and the stress goes up and this cycle spins down until you feel utterly exhausted.

The cycle of overflow recognizes that all the love we give comes from ourselves. We can only love, give and serve if we ourselves are full. Our first priority is to take care of ourselves. We don't have the ability to control others, take away their pain or save them from their burdens, but we do have the autonomy to ensure that at least one person in their world is doing okay – and that is us.

We start giving to us. We make sure we are okay.

When we keep giving ourselves what we need, this is what happens: we become so full of love, we overflow. We naturally share our love with others. We feel so good that we want the same for those around us.

This is the cycle of overflow.

Autonomy Is Strength

You are a person who is rich, full of wonder, power and desire. You have the ability to trust that desire and go after it.

But often we don't. We neglect ourselves. We ignore ourselves. We despise ourselves. We distract from ourselves.

And in our eternal exodus from ourselves, we look toward others for our sense of self.

In a relationship, rather than trusting who you are, what you want, what you are here for, you look at your partner. What does he want? What energy is he bringing to the exchange?

Instead of taking the courage to make a decision about a really exciting idea that motivates you, you ask, "What do *you* want to do?" Instead of thinking about a solution that will solve the problem to your satisfaction, taking into account who you are and what will make you feel cared for, you ask, "What do *you* think we should do?"

Instead of making your life a celebration of the glorious person you are, you make it about others. Where are the Jones going on vacation? What are the values they are imbuing in their children? What do "they" say I should wear, do, care about or date? I should do that, too.

We farm out our lives into the hands of other people.

When you do that, I can predict this: someone will let you down. Because nobody can hold your heart the way you can. And it's not their job.

The problem is, you've outsourced your happiness. Now you cannot afford to have someone else lose, abuse or forget your heart. So now that you are in their hands, you start obsessing over them.

You check to see if your spouse is in a good mood. You survey a room right when you walk in, to take the temperature and check if it's safe. You say the words you know the other person wishes to hear. You dress and act in ways that others approve. You endure parties, activities or causes that are near to other's hearts, because you believe you need to curry favor with them. You must now be their indentured servant, because they have your heart, and you are protecting it.

Autonomy means you know you will be okay no matter what happens in your relationships. Humans are fallible and they may fail you, but they can't truly hurt you, because they don't have that power. You have the power to protect you, and you honor that to the best of your ability. This frees you up to be you, to love everything in the world that you love.

It frees you up to love others as they are, not as a steward of your safety and wellbeing, but as themselves, human and imperfect beings. And it frees the other person up to be himself.

That person may be in a bad mood one day. It happens. But it doesn't threaten your safety because you will be fine. That person may have had a very difficult experience. You can be there for him, because his experience doesn't threaten yours.

You can be there as a resource. You can trust that he will make it through. You don't need to fall apart on his behalf. You can trust his process. You are free.

Things may happen – disappointments, hard times, distractions. You can always center yourself back into your heart, your mind, your body, the loves and desires you have. Autonomy is your strength.

Autonomy and Boundaries

Fences make poor boundaries. You can make fences, but you can't keep someone else's smog out. You can build walls, but you can't keep their voices out. You can erect barriers, but you can't keep their attitudes from snaking through.

Autonomy, as an effective alternative, offers you the ability to stand in someone else's reality and choose *you*. You choose what *you* need to survive and thrive. You choose how *you* want to interact. You choose what impact *you* want to have on the world. You take into account that we are inexorably linked, and you act in integrity with yourself.

In a relationship where the other person is disrespectful, you don't have the ability to change that person. But you sure can decide what you want to do and how you want to respond.

Most important, you can know how it affects you.

Without knowing how it affects you, you don't know how to respond. You respond from instinct. You either respond in the moment, from a place of great pain and little power, or you don't respond at all, choosing to deny, minimize, focus on other things, or just forget it. When you can simply hold inside of you the experience of how you are being affected, you can then deal with it. You don't need to pretend it isn't there. You don't need to judge yourself, to think if you had been stronger, had better boundaries, been wiser or more selfless, you wouldn't have been in this place. You simply acknowledge that human beings have a direct impact on one another. Since you are in direct line of another human being's behavior, this is the experience of it. You acknowledge it. You feel it. You own it.

When you don't judge what happened to you, the other person loses the power and hold over you. You see things clearly. When, in a relationship, the other person hurts and then apologizes, again and again, you are not at the mercy of his moods and whims. You have your own truth.

How to Develop Autonomy

Step 1 – Get Back to Your Reality

Autonomy is being able to act from your seat of power. What is your seat of power?

You. You courageously embracing all of who you are. All your desires. All your emotions. All your limitations. All of it.

I told my friend Ciri that I used to suffer greatly from existential shame. She responded, "But you're so confident. It comes naturally to you." I laughed, because I knew. She saw me now. She hadn't known me then.

I couldn't convince her. Maybe if she'd been with me at that wedding. My neighbor's son was getting married. I had gone over and exchanged pleasantries and small talk with many people. Some of the guests intimidated me, so I stayed on the sidelines, avoiding them because I felt like I didn't know what to say. I hoped they didn't notice me avoid them, that they didn't notice me at all.

And now that I was walking down the cobblestoned hill toward home, I wanted to rip myself apart. I saw myself eating from the dessert table, so awkwardly. I saw myself talking to people, saying the wrong things. I saw myself, and I hated myself.

The big question that tormented me was, "What were they thinking about me?"

The probable answers were scary. And because that had become more important than what I was thinking about myself, I felt powerless and crazed as I considered the possibilities through their lens.

My mother had once told me, "Are you worried about what others think about you? Don't worry. They're all thinking about themselves."

But I knew there were people like me, people who had no sense of self and preferred witnessing another's pain and downfall rather than facing their own. I was turning to that entire ecosystem of people feeding off each other, and it left me wondering if I had misstepped in their eyes.

When I decided to turn my life around, the first thing I did was draw the lines. This is who I am. I am Chany Rosengarten. I am not all those other people. I am not my cousin, I am not my neighbor. I am not the cool kid. I am not in their heads. I don't have to consider their thoughts.

At a more recent wedding I found myself doing it again. It was a family wedding, and I started to doubt myself. Had I been weird? Said something funny? What did they think of me? Did my great aunt, Tanta Mimi, the child therapist, talk to my daughter because she wanted to, because she felt obligated to, or because she felt pity for my child? I felt lost inside of me, like I no longer wanted to be associated with myself.

The first thing I did was redraw the lines: This is who I am.

Did I wear the right outfit? I forced myself out of my elegant aunt's mind and back into my body. This is the dress I chose to wear. I could feel it. I patted the seams at the waist. I remembered why I had chosen to wear it. *Because I liked it.*

Did I say the right things to the right people? I drew myself out from where I had buried my tentacles of self-doubt. I was not living in my aunt's mind.

Did I always make the best choices? My choices were my own. They were good enough. Would my family members have chosen differently? Definitely. They would have. But that's because they were them. For me, no better choices existed, because we always choose the best choice from among the ones we have.

Once the lines were drawn, I at least knew who I was. That felt good.

Inside of who I am, I could allow myself to make mistakes. I allowed myself to do what *they* thought I shouldn't do. I allowed myself to be me.

That's autonomy. It's the ability to hold our own truth, to operate from our own internal compass.

Step 2 - Recognize Your Power

In any relationship, there is I, and there is the other person. All relationships are an agreement between two people.

One of those two people is you. The other person is your partner in the interaction.

Because you are focused on relating to the other person, the spotlight is on that person. You look at them and away from yourself. You talk to them. You listen to them. You feel them out.

In all the focus on the person you interact with, you forget one simple thing: you are doing all the relating.

In most normal interactions, we are so focused on the other person that we forget ourselves. The interaction is natural to us: we are so habituated to relate, that we forget ourselves, much like we forget to think about buttoning our clothes: it simply happens.

You'll know this to be true because there are times, such as when you need to speak to a crowd, go to an interview, talk to someone you revere, or post yourself talking on social media, when it doesn't come naturally. Those times are uncomfortable because you are self-conscious. You are conscious of yourself, more than you are conscious of the other person. You go from forgetting yourself in the interaction to monitoring your every nuance.

While we usually forget ourselves in a normal interaction, we don't forget the other person. That person requires our attention because we don't know how he will respond to our input. That's why it's easy to forget that we are at least fifty percent of the interaction.

If you are able to change your awareness and focus on your part in the interaction, it gives you a really large part in what is happening. You can now control the rules of the interaction. You can't control what the other person is doing, ever. But you do have leverage, as a majority owner in this interaction.

Why is this important?

It gives you all the power you need to have interactions that serve you well.

This simple fact has given women of all ages the ability to leave toxic relationships, rewrite existing ones, and create powerful, self-actualizing relationships with partners at their level.

I want to remind you that relationships should feel wonderful, affirm who you are, and honor you. You have a whole, large, complex and beautiful life that includes your history, your future, your dreams, your relationships ... and the person who is interacting with you has the same thing, an entire universe that keeps him alive and supported, and provides him with perspective.

When you maintain awareness of an interaction, you can ask yourself a simple question: Is this interaction serving you?

Because if it is demeaning you, overlooking you, or giving you a feeling that is less than affirming, it's time to ever so subtly, ever so powerfully, change the dynamic.

We can't change anything that the other person does. We wish we could, and we spend a lot of energy on changing others. We explain. We label them with names and couch diagnoses. We beg. We threaten. Oh, what don't we do when we are in a relationship with someone we wish would be behaving differently! But that's not within our ability. As humans, we can only change ourselves.

There is power in that recognition. Yes, it feels pointless. I'm not the one who needs to change. He's the one who is causing all this heartache.

Yet by remembering that you have a one hundred percent stake in the relationship, just as your partner does, you get to come back to yourself and take care of the one area where you do have enormous power: you.

Step 3 – Controlling Only Yourself

Rather than looking towards your partner and waiting for him to change, take the courage to change yourself.

You can change how you respond. You can walk away from a painful conversation. You don't need to prove that you deserve better because you are not looking to change the other person, anyway. You simply remove yourself.

You can also say something new.

Let's look at a conversation with your colleague.

He's not being respectful. You realize you have a full stake in this conversation, so you're not going to let him talk down at you. Not on your watch.

You have two choices. One is to say, "I'll get rid of this right now." You barge in and fight the guy to death. You're trying to bring him down, to quash his behavior so it doesn't happen again. You're not taking garbage from anyone anymore. Not you, not ever.

The other choice is to recognize yourself in this interaction. You've been allowing disrespectful communication for a while. That's very painful. There's a lot riding on your ability to stop this, in this one conversation.

Bravery would be acknowledging all of this pain. And yet knowing that you are here for it.

When you recognize just how big your actions are, you can take smaller ones, because you know that they are courageous. If you know how much one step can move you forward, you don't need to climb the whole mountain.

You're standing next to your colleague who just disrespected you. And you say, "What you just said made me feel disrespected."

Has anyone ever said that to him, in this way, from a place of personal ownership and power? Probably not.

This gives him pause.

He opens his eyes. He sees you in a new light. He sees that you are not taking his garbage and ignoring it, or shutting down, or lashing back.

He may see that, in your quiet courage, you mean business.

"I'm sorry," he says. Or maybe he doesn't. Maybe he's too taken aback by this new interaction. But he feels a new feeling. He has space to look at himself, because you aren't. All you're doing is looking after yourself.

You don't say, "It's okay." You don't because you know that it wasn't okay. You know how brave you were to just say what you want. How hard this was.

So you say, "Thank you." In that thanks you recognize his own bravery.

That's it. The dynamics have shifted. You now own how this conversation will go, in the present, and in the future.

All you said was something so simple. His words, too, did not seek to eliminate years of conditioning. And it's enough. In this small interaction, you have stood up for yourself and shifted years of ways of being. And all it took was a small change.

You didn't spew eloquence. You didn't imagine that he overflowed with hatred. You were in your power. You knew you had autonomy over this situation, because it was *your* situation. You weren't cowed by how it has been done until now. You didn't hate yourself for not having it done differently until this moment. You were in your power. That's autonomy.

Chapter 5

The Third Step – Negotiation

How comfortable are you asking for your needs?

For most of us, the answer ranges from "not very" to "not at all" with a few "I know how to fight for my needs."

But none of these is knowing how to negotiate for your needs.

Saying it's okay when it's not okay, not at all, is one way of not being able to ask for your needs.

But so is fighting for your needs.

Negotiation is asking for your needs, clearly and concisely. Negotiation is trusting that you deserve to have your needs met. You know that *you* have a responsibility to advocate for yourself, and so you do. You ask for what you need and trust that you will get it.

Negotiation is where we advocate for ourselves because we trust that we deserve to receive.

Taking Care of You

Before we had autonomy, we believed that if we only took great care of others, they would take really good care of us. We didn't think it was important to state our needs. We assumed that if we are taking care of them, or sacrificing for them, it is implied that they would take great pains to figure out what we needed and give it to us.

The stereotype goes something like this: a woman waits for her husband to buy her a birthday present. He asks her what she wants, but she doesn't want to say. "If I have to ask for it, it doesn't really count. You should *know*."

But when you have autonomy, you know it's no one's direct responsibility to give it to you. That's your responsibility, and you'd better do a good job of it.

On the other hand, you don't need to take care of your every need by yourself, just as you don't need to plant your wheat, harvest it, grind it into flour and bake your own bread. Others can do it for you. It's your job to negotiate for it.

You need to ask for your needs clearly. That's your way of taking care of yourself in a relationship. That's the next step after autonomy.

Often, we wait for others to take care of us without having the courage to ask for it because we don't really believe we can get it. We avoid asking for a raise because deep down, we think we should just be satisfied with what we already have. We avoid asking for love because it feels too painful if our request won't be honored.

We shun asking for clarity in a relationship ("What exactly is going on, are we committed, why are you avoiding me?") because we think we can tolerate the pain of being in vagueness.

When we know how deserving we are, we have the courage to ask for what we need. We know that we may not get our requests answered right away, and that's okay. But asking is the first step in honoring our needs.

Business and Personal

With all this talk about negotiation, you may be thinking you are preparing for battle. Negotiations are generally used in the context of business or politics, not in close relationships or easy friendships. If Apple is going to partner with Nike for their watches, or with Mastercard for their payment processing, they very clearly know that they are both doing it to benefit their bottom line. The business has a good sense of self; it knows its boundaries. If a business is going to pool resources with another entity, clear ideas of why and how they are working together must be established.

Now that you have established autonomy and have a clear awareness that you, too, are an entity, you can see why your conversations need to be based in clarity. You need to take care of your interests so you can run at optimal capacity. If a country fails at negotiation, it might be facing war, famine, invasion or diminished resources. If your conversations are conducted in a way that doesn't care for you, what is the fallout?

For me, not advocating for myself was my ultimate downfall. There was that time I was on the phone with my aunt, a cramp ripping through my stomach. She was talking, she had a lot to say during that conversation ... none of which I remember.

All I remember was the crippling inability to be clear about the fact that I needed to go, that my time was mine, that I was no longer available for the conversation. Instead, I danced, I swayed like I was in labor but not yet ready to deliver the baby, I bit my lip, I prayed for relief... and I stayed in the conversation.

That's a small story with little to no repercussions. Would my aunt have been accepting if I said something as simple as, "I need to go now, let's continue this conversation tomorrow"? Probably. I know that personally, I prefer someone honor my time by being honest about hers if she can't talk now.

But there were instances of much greater damage that stemmed from my inability to communicate clearly. My marriage, for example. If I couldn't hang up the phone mid-conversation, do you think I was able to say no to what felt uncomfortable, and yes to what I wanted? I didn't recognize that even inside of a close relationship that I greatly cherished, I could have a self, and that self could communicate her wants very clearly.

Instead, I said things like, "Okay, if that's what you want." Had someone been experienced in deciphering cryptic messages, he would have understood that "okay" means, *I don't want to, but what choice do I have in the face of your wanting, so I'll just agree so as not to have to go through a conversation in which I do the difficult task of negotiating for myself,* and "if that's what you want" meant, *Do you really, really want that? Because this is a big deal for me, and I'm only doing it to please you. Make sure you want this with your entire being, because otherwise, the self sacrifice I am doing is going to go largely unnoticed, and that would be tragic, as the only reason I'm doing it is for you.* My husband just took my words at face value.

I agreed to a lot of things I didn't want to agree to. I expected my husband to honor my sacrificial offerings, but he was blind to them. My resentments grew.

I went without a lot of my needs. I couldn't ask for them, but I also couldn't go without them. Instead, I withdrew, sent out desperate distress signals in the form of passive aggressive gestures, and felt alone and uncared for.

We all silence ourselves sometimes. We cram into old ways that don't fit. We pinch our needs like petulant children who just want things at the most inopportune times, and instead of indulging in our desperate tantrums, we try acting like stoic adults. We silence ourselves because it's easier than honoring our needs enough to see them through.

I remember when I started practicing being honest about my needs and just communicating them. It was the bravest thing I ever did.

When I asked for my needs, I asked for them plainly. Stated my needs, stated how I was going to attend to them, asked for the specific help I needed.

I'm still practicing negotiation. I still don't always ask for what I need. There are parts of me that would rather stay silenced because I believe I don't deserve it. When I find myself going into resentment or passive aggressive behavior, I know that there is a need here that is begging for attention, while the stoic part of me stands in front of her, not letting her be.

I listen and ask, "Sweetie, what do you need?" My answer is, "I need attention." A big part of me is ashamed for wanting it. Still, I go to the next step. "Can I ask for that?" If I can, my misery is stopped.

I wanted to eat out one Sunday evening. My husband hates restaurants. I love them. My favorite thing is sitting down at a small brown table and being served a meal that an excellent and creative chef has cooked up for me. Because otherwise, it's me being the creative chef, standing over pots and sautéing, stirring, and serving. For my husband, restaurants are just another way of being served food, except with an added wait time and inflated bill.

We wanted to have a nice time together. He said, "What should we do?"

I had a hard time saying, "I'd really like to eat out tonight." I was ready to say, "I don't know," which is my cop out when I don't feel brave enough to know.

I was thinking about his perspective. His probable answer, once I would tell him what I wanted. Why eating out was not fun or important when I could just pack sandwiches and we could go somewhere interesting for both of us. And so it went on, about two hundred thoughts fighting against my one desire to eat out.

But I'm brave. So I told him I'd like to eat out. He did say the things I thought he'd say. But he agreed and we went and it was really nice.

In real time, the conversation went like this.

Him: "What should we do tonight?"

Me: "I'd like to eat out at a restaurant."

Him: "But we can just eat at home and then go somewhere. All right, let's do it. Which restaurant?"

I won't bore you with the mind games that happened over this next question. But the point is, the conversation doesn't need to be clumsy when we do all the heavy lifting inside of ourselves.

How to Succeed in Negotiation

Step 1 – Know What You Want

To have the outcome you want, you must know what you want. Otherwise, how will you know if you got what you wanted?

This is so obvious that we often overlook it. But when you enter any interaction, do you know what it is that you want from that interaction? Do you even realize that you have permission to want something? Even if this situation is good for you, you still have permission to want more.

How often do we negotiate with ourselves, haggling over our own happiness as if we have to ration it? We ask ourselves: Why aren't you happy with what you have? Shouldn't this be enough? If I get a really good thing, won't I need to give up something else? Am I even allowed to enjoy this largesse? We downplay our needs: I'm only doing this for my partner, I would be happy with much less. I am so virtuous for undergoing all this suffering. I'm not going to expect anything because I'm satisfied. I'm healthy, after all, and there are people who are not. I have a warm meal, and children in Africa would leap at the chance to eat the scraps …

Sound familiar? The first step in any negotiation where your own needs are taken into account is knowing that you do, indeed, deserve to have your needs met.

When I started writing, I was so excited about my ability to write and be heard, I would have paid the magazines to publish my story. The fact that it was the other way around made me feel indebted, to the point where I'd sell myself off into slavery for my editors. Had I known to care for the precious, gifted writer that I was, I would have noticed the talent I was bringing to the table. I would have appreciated my writing just as they did. I would have known that no prestigious magazine worth their pages publish articles to do favors for the writer; they publish articles because they are good, because I was good. I would have known that I write well and was deserving of being paid.

One day my editor asked if I'd write a serial novel. Of course I would. This was a dream come true. I had worked my way up in the writing world with the dream of writing a serial novel. It seemed unattainable. And now I was asked to write one, for the top magazine in my industry.

The editor named a price per installment that she was willing to pay. "Is that okay with you?" she asked.

My response: *Are you kidding me*? I was overjoyed. I was in no position to negotiate a better rate, even though her question revealed that she was expecting me to negotiate. I just took what she gave me and ran, before she changed her mind and asked me to pay her for the privilege.

And truthfully, the amount of money was fine.

My lack of belief in myself wasn't helpful, not for me, not for my editor. Because in not advocating for myself, I was also saying, "I don't believe I'm that good of a writer. I think it is a great privilege to write for you. Such a great privilege that it even scares me."

I was scared. I'd sit on my coach for hours, tormenting every word as it squeezed its way through my fingers. I experienced writer's block, or to be more accurate, writer's paralysis. The novel was mediocre at best.

Several years later, having learned to value myself, my time, my gifts and my needs, I was asked to write a serialized novel again. This time, I asked for a deserving payment. In honoring my craft, I wrote from a place of power. That novel (which became my Amazon bestseller, *Promise Me Jerusalem*) has since touched the lives of many, and it lives on beyond the time I made a decision to ask for my needs.

It's hard to know what we want. Even when we do get a small inkling, it's hard to trust that it's okay to want what we want. But it's important to enter a conversation from a place of knowing what we want, so the outcome is what we want.

This can be surprisingly challenging. Life is complex. How are you supposed to know what you want when it conflicts with other things you want, or with your feelings, or with your desire to please?

A lot of people who desperately need to give themselves time, or care, or receive compassion and love, call themselves egotistical and selfish when they contemplate actually asking for what they need. They can't think beyond what everyone else needs.

One Friday, my to-do list was so long, it looked like a receipt. I was overwhelmed and angry, sluggishly going from task to task. Then I decided to take everyone and everything out of the picture and ask myself, "What do you want, sweetie?" And listen, compassionately, to the answer. That's it.

It turned out I needed some time outside of the kitchen, out in the world far beyond my little family. I took a long drive. I was out for an hour. You know what happened?

Everything else got taken care of.

Through my brave questioning and compassionate answering, I honed in on one thing I really needed:

space. By taking it, I was also taking care of everything else.

You can trust your desires. They are not there to trip you up, make you selfish, or entice you with the impossible. Your desires are sacred maps, your soul's way of pulling you forward into the future.

Can you trust that? Can you hear yourself clearly now, above the din of the chorus that wants to shut you down?

Step 2 - Ask for It

Now that you know what you want, you can clearly communicate your expectations.

Communicating the outcome you desire is your next step. There are many volumes and shelves dedicated to effective communication. I won't tell you how to communicate. Because it doesn't matter. The more complex we try to be with our delivery, the further we are from the truth of what we want.

I have one rule in communication: Be honest. Take a deep breath and be brave. Just say it. Say it simply. Say it clumsily. Just say what you want. And if something other than what you want comes out of your mouth (because it can be so hard to tell the truth when it comes to your needs, your limitations and your values), you can say it again, but clearer this time. You can take as many tries as you'd like. You can forgive yourself for how you've said things. But the thing must be said.

Congratulations on your bravery.

Step 3 - Silence

Step three: stop. Just stay silent. This is the part where you rest on your laurels. You know you've done the deep work, the work of knowing what you want and communicating it. Now, you are quiet.

You don't explain.

You don't defend yourself.

You don't beg.

You don't add caveats.

You don't say, "But it's okay. It's what I want, but I totally get why you wouldn't ..."

You just breathe, shut your lips super tight, and relax all the areas in your body that feel like they want to scream.

This is the great pause. Listen to your vulnerability. You are feeling raw. Angry. Desperate. Pause and honor those emotions. Let them swim up, wash over you, and trust that they will recede. You've done great work. That in itself is enough.

Step 4 - Trust the Process

When I was a little kid, my school offered about eight different lunches. One was a fish patty, deep fried until it resembled a little black rock. The inside, however, was fluffy and white and sweet and delicious. But nobody dared to eat it. We had nicknames for the fish. We called it poop. We made fun of the kids eating it. But I really liked it.

Tuna was also not in vogue. If you ate the tuna instead of turning up your nose at it, you were nerdy. At least with the tuna, I was in luck. I dislike tuna salad until today. But the fish patties were a different story. They were so good. I still hunger for the patties I didn't dare eat then.

It's funny how certain foods became verboten because the first kid or two turned up their noses against them. And certain foods, like pasta, were totally permissible, even though I still can't fathom how I ate pasta smothered in ketchup, or in cocoa and sugar. But at that time, there were very clear unspoken rules. Pasta in ketchup, the whole class ate. Fish patties? Nobody was hungry that day.

I think in some ways I'm still that little kid. I'm still afraid to enjoy what life offers me, literally on a plate served directly to me, because of what others might say. The bravest thing I've done is to dig into what I want and go after it. You know what happened in high school, when I finally had the courage to eat the fish? Some kids made a face, others followed suit, but the best part? I had a good lunch.

You may have an easy time asking for your needs. In fact, you may be so direct, you almost border on aggression. There were areas in my life where my asking did not look at all vulnerable. I was ready to fight as needed. Ironically, those were the areas in my life where I least believed I deserved to receive.

When you think you won't get something that you hunger for, you grab, you are aggressive, you push. Have you ever eaten a meal when you were famished? I have, and I know what it looks like. I get clumsy. I eat entire swallows at a time. I hurry.

Following the steps of negotiation is just as important for those of us who appear extra macho. Believe that you deserve it, whether you can get it right now or not. Even if people have historically denied you, remember that if you have the desire for it, you deserve it.

Ask it plainly. You don't need to bring in the big guns. Just state your desire. The fact that you have asked demonstrates trust that you deserve. And if you've been brave enough to state your needs, you will most likely get it. Trust that.

Step 5 – Let Go

Through your asking, one thing has become clear – you know what you want. You know that if you want it, you can ask for it. You are open to receiving it.

Yet the fact that you are ready to receive it doesn't mean that the person on the other side is ready to give it.

Diamonds didn't fall from the sky once I started communicating. My spouse didn't always want the thing I wanted. Having felt completely vulnerable making my needs known, I now felt wounded. But placing your wellbeing in the hands of one, limited person was never in your best interest. And you are now pursuing your own best interest.

So even if the person you are negotiating with is your husband, your boss, your client or your child, he is not the only one with the ability to help you. Believing that he is compromises your resources, affecting your confidence in stating your needs. Open up. The world is full of amazing resources. If you are ready for something, it will come.

This knowing allows you to let go of the one person you asked your need from. And in that freedom, you have the confidence to say your truth. You can ask for what you want and take care of your emotions as you wait.

Step 6 – Listen

Now it's time to listen. Listen to how the other person responds. See his desire to give, or his sense of frustration at his inability to give.

When you know you've done your part in advocating for yourself, you can listen without an agenda. You know you have done your part, which is to clarify what you need, and verbalize it. You trust that you will get it, whether this person can give it to you or not. Now you are ready to listen.

Listen well. Hear the other person explain. Or defend. Or come toward you to meet you. Or lovingly provide you with the needs you've asked for. You'll start noticing the love you've always had but never received. You'll start experiencing the respect that was always there but you couldn't hold. You'll start hearing the truth.

Step 7 - Repeat the Steps, Refining the Process

And if in due time, when the other person has run out of responses and you find you need to say more, you will go back to step one. What do you want now?

Consider the new information. You'll go from there, expressing your needs, asking for them, waiting, attending to your own feelings, trusting, letting go of them, listening.

Practice asking for your needs. Practice it so it becomes natural to you, so you can ease into the fact that we all need each other.

Ask for something small. Or big. Whatever it is that you really need.

State what your need is, and then stay quiet. Watch your benefactor tell you why he can or can't provide. Don't make excuses, don't say it's okay. You don't need to dramatize how important it is to you. Just stay in the space of knowing your request and asking for it.

How do you feel?

Are you comfortable asking for what you need?

Can you see that as you negotiate for your needs, you establish for yourself who you are, and what you want? That is your boundary.

Chapter 6

The Fourth Step – Direction

What is direction? It begins with having a vision. It's knowing what you want and heading that way.

Direction is the permission to pick a desire and pursue it. Direction is finding your purpose and passion and taking steps towards it. It's the central motivation for who you are.

Direction is the ability to choose your path. Your path may be very connected to people, but it's not because of people. It's because of you.

Why is this important? Because when you know where you are going, you are not stuck in another person's reality. You can each be yourself. You can both thrive and co-exist.

Direction means knowing your desires and pursuing it. That's a life worth living. Trust that your desires are good. They will not lead you astray. And trust that you deserve a good life.

Sometimes life takes us into pretty difficult places. I know. I've been there. I was so embroiled in the life that wasn't working, that envisioning a life with all the things I wanted was a painful tease. Now, I map out my vision. I get clear on my desires going forward. And then I take small steps toward it.

Sometimes, that step is an outside thing. I need to take action. The action can be small. A phone call. Googling a question. Taking a nap. Sometimes the action isn't an action at all, but a pause. A knowledge that I've clarified my desires, and by doing so, I am on my way.

The Road to Joy

Want to be filled with joy and vitality?

You're not going to find that inside another person. But don't give up looking ... it's closer than you think. You will find that joy in you.

When you are stuck in the pain of living according to another's desires, you can't be free and you can't be happy. As soon as you've made the decision to honor your own vision, your world opens up with options for joy.

We each have different desires which are tailored directly to our life mission. Following those desires allows us to map out our destiny. If we listen to that internal nudge, we will find that we have accomplished a life with many wonderful and varied experiences. We'll be fulfilling our mission.

If you are overwhelmed, stuck in someone else's story, or feeling lethargic in your day to day living, it's time to pick your own direction. You may feel clueless right now, or you may feel like just thinking about mapping your own way is painful and exhausting.

But you should know that your options are truly open and unlimited.

The ten people around you who have similar desires to yours are not reflective of your range of choices in this world. More exist.

The addictions you may have been using to numb the pain of avoiding your life's direction is not your desire, and certainly do not lead to joy.

For me, food was a balm. I didn't have self-respect, but at least I could fill my tummy with soothing ice cream, chocolate and smoothies.

Technology was another blanket. I could always turn to the computer. If nothing interesting was there, I would refresh the screen one more time and lose myself in the steel blue of the computer's glare.

I still ate chocolate after I clarified my real direction. But it had lost its romance. It still tasted good, but it no longer had its grip.

Now is the time to be intentional about your life. You deserve to take out of this life experience exactly what you hoped you'd get. You may want to open yourself up to surprises and new discoveries along the way. But before you do, create a picture in your mind so you know what you are hoping to get to.

Setting Your Life's GPS

A GPS gives you directions. It doesn't take you there, but if you follow the road mapped out for you, you will get from where you are to where you want to be. If you start out in New York and you're heading toward Florida, the first turn onto the highway doesn't mean you're there yet. All you have is a car and a plan. The plan is enough. If you keep going long enough in that car with those directions, you will find that you have arrived.

All you need is direction. Direction makes you into the person you want to be. It gives you a solid boundary in this world full of people who want a part of you. it reminds you of who *you* are and who *you* want to be.

There was a time in my life when I knew exactly what everyone else wanted from me. My life was filled with these varied roles. I was a daughter to my mother. And to my father. I was a sister to my brothers. And to my sisters. I was a friend to various friends, each one expecting me to fulfill her friendship needs. I was an employee. I was a mother. I was a neighbor. I was a community member.

My plate was full. Too overflowing for me to wonder, what do I want for me?

But also: I was feeling dead. I felt burdened and exhausted and despite investing my entire life into others, I was coming up short. I could never lose the emptiness of not having a self.

I never asked myself, "Sweetie, what do you want?"

When I was living in deep avoidance of myself, steeped in the pursuit of making other people happy, I thought we all had the same desires. Mine were a reflection of other people's. If they thought wearing expensive, tailored, imported clothing was important, it became important to me. It became a pursuit, because in attaining those clothes, I would reflect their ideals. I'd wear a fur-edged satin suit and they would admire my look. Then they would like me. All would be well.

But when I got honest with myself about what I wanted, it wasn't what they wanted. It took bravery for me to say that I wanted to write, to teach, to be vocal, because I was afraid people would say, "Who does she think she is?"

And here is who I finally think I am. Chany Rosengarten, heart, body and soul.

How to Clarify Your Direction

Step One – Identify Your Dreams

If you could have the life you really want, and it would be beautiful and possible, what would it look like?

Dream a little. You may want to put the book down. You may want to fantasize here. You may want to rush ahead, because who likes to think about what you want when you are so far away from it? But bear with me, and forgive yourself if you can't, because we are about to dig deep, and you may discover that the life worth living is the life that is yours.

Here are some questions.

1.What is making you really uncomfortable? What would you like to be different?

_____

_____

_____

_____

_____

_____

_____

2.What do you believe you deserve but have never taken the courage to get?

_____

_____

_____

_____

_____

_____

_____

3.What area in your life would be different with the proper attention and support?

_____

_____

_____

_____

_____

_____

4.What will change when you are a fully empowered and confident person?

_____

_____

_____

_____

_____

_____

5.What will create disappointment in you if you don't change?

_____

_____

_____

_____

_____

_____

6. What is your vision, your hope, as you create a sense of self?

_____

_____

_____

_____

_____

_____

7. Identify a person who seems to have it all. What does she have? What do you want?

_____

_____

_____

_____

_____

_____

It doesn't matter if your dreams seem attainable. What's important is that you are honest about them.

How often do we sternly tell ourselves not to dream, because what happens if they don't come true? Here's a simple truth: they definitely won't come true if you don't even allow yourself to want it.

So want it. Admit it. That's it.

Direction doesn't mean you have it all figured out. As you travel down a road, what was around the bend reveals itself. You couldn't have seen it at the beginning of your journey. Direction is knowing where you want to go, and setting out on the journey.

Step Two – Make it Real

Now that you've considered your ideal outcome, it's time to solidify it. Write it out. Share it with at least one person, because saying it out loud crystalizes the commitment for you and makes it real.

Write a list. Write it all out. Now it's tangible. it's real.

Next, make it memorable. Think of one word that describes the feeling you will have once you have accomplished all the desires on your list. In your day to day living, it can be hard to stay focused on where you want to go, because there are so many things right in front of you that need to get done. But if you have one word, a feeling that encompasses all that you want for yourself, that's something you can remember. It's your code word for yourself.

This word is your vision. Keep it where you can see it every day. Review it. Remember it. It's yours. You may be bogged down by pressing things now, but hey, you are going somewhere, and you're headed in the right direction.

Step Three – Take the First Step

Start taking micro-steps in the direction of your dream. Just one step. Just once a week. Just for fifteen minutes.

I have a dream of owning a beautiful home, with lovely spaces. I've had that dream ever since I moved out of my first apartment, which I had decorated with lush white carpets, gold embroidered linens and jugs of flowers. When I moved across the globe, and then subsequently back to New York, both times I neglected to decorate my space in a way that reflected my tastes and comfort. I was too busy surviving. Instead, I dreamed about the mansion that would be tailored to my fantasies.

But it never happened.

Eventually I exhausted myself waiting, and decided to just start now. I had a long list of things I wanted. Carpets and drapes, sunlight and trees, lush grass and views. What would I feel when I had all of that? I would feel a deep sense of serenity that comes with being present in my own space. Aha! That was my vision. My vision was serenity. What micro-steps could I take, even if I didn't live in a mansion yet?

Remarkably, the world became full of opportunity.

My porch became a haven. I started appreciating the landscape around my apartment, which included many of the things on my list. I actually already had lush grass, rose bushes and hydrangeas growing right under my window. I bought some lovely paintings and a jute rug, and hung a chandelier. They were smaller steps than my grand dream, but they gave me a home, and I experienced serenity.

We all have these big, unattainable dreams. We think we need to achieve those dreams to finally have the life we want. But in truth, it's the little actions we take every day that are aligned with our vision which propel us in the direction we want to go. If we do the tiny actions, one day we wake up and find we are living inside of our dream.

You may be very busy with all the things that pull at you, possibly based on other people's desires. Take the time to take one step in the direction of you. Affirm to yourself that this is where you are headed.

Chapter 7

Bringing Back Your
Sense of Self

By now you know why boundaries are so essential. Boundaries give us the ability to love. In the absence of needing to carry the burden of the other's emotional wellbeing, we open up to being more fully present in the relationship, as ourselves.

Boundaries give us safety. When we have full permission to be ourselves, we can be real. We aren't needlessly respecting someone to the point where we disrespect ourselves. We know that it's our job to care for ourselves so we say what we feel and need.

Boundaries give us intimacy. When we don't see closeness as one person overlapping the other, we can both get as close as we can, while still retaining our individuality. We see the other person as the other, thus heightening the thrill of connection.

Boundaries give us respect. When we own the entirety of who we are, we don't sell out so fast to anyone else's opinion. We hold our own with confidence and surety.

Boundaries give us what we want. We know what we want and need and respect our desires. We have poise in the process of waiting for our needs to be fulfilled because we recognize the need and we are willing to honor it. We trust that our needs will be fulfilled.

Loving ourselves, asserting our autonomy, negotiating for our needs and finding our direction is the way to shift dynamics from the inside out.

How Are My Boundaries Doing?

How do we know that we need to strengthen our boundaries? What are the signs that it's time to reinforce our sense of self?

We each have specific times in our lives when we instinctively feel the need to regain equilibrium inside the interdependent family relationship. These are important developmental milestones that are essential for your balance as an individual within connectedness. The terrible twos, as well as your teenage years, are examples of these volatile times. The developing you needs to pull away from its dependency on others and practice individuality within the framework of family. By leaning against the parameters of loving relationships and pushing as far as you can go, you gain a deep experience of your individuality supported by love.

Sometimes these stages are misunderstood, and the individual's attempts at rebelling are quickly quelled. If this was your experience, it left you with two choices: either forget about being an individual, forget yourself and become "the good child," or rebel completely, be rejected, misunderstood and alone, and cling to your fragile sense of self as if you, and only you, have all the answers.

Both of these choices are painful. Choosing to stay squashed within the family system leaves you with weak, porous boundaries. Having forgotten who you are, you tend to grow into adulthood as a deeply dependent person, attracting partners who either need your help or will save you. Choosing to rebel and risking the ire of your family leaves you with the mistaken belief that connection as an individual is impossible. If you ever want to connect, you'll believe it will always be at your own expense, so you frequently choose to stay away from intimate situations that might compromise your identity. You believe that you are deeply flawed and unlovable, and also solely responsible for your own wellbeing.

The reality of living in this world is that you will encounter trauma, and it will affect you. Understanding that you were affected, that your boundaries were violated, that you forgot who you are, understanding the story of how it happened, offers you an opportunity to mend that rift and get back into your own glorious body and life.

Steps to a Sense of Self

Step One – Admit It

If you are not feeling good about yourself, stop and admit it to yourself.

"I'm feeling really lousy right now. I'm telling myself that I am stupid, horrible, ugly or unwanted."

Can we stay here a minute and just breathe? That took courage. It's hard to be feeling it and to be honest about feeling it.

Most of us dump a lot of garbage right on top of a bad feeling. We feel bad about ourselves, so we go eat, starve ourselves for the day, work long and grueling hours, take revenge, or do any of the other things that will cover up a bad feeling with a worse feeling so the initial truth of how we felt doesn't surface. It's easier to blame and hate ourselves for saying or doing the wrong thing than to tolerate the negative feelings we have about ourselves.

If you are brave enough to admit that, yeah, I'm feeling lousy right now, you are with self. That's pretty brave.

Step Two – Go Back in Time

Think of a time in your past that you felt this way. This feeling isn't new. In fact, the reason it's so intolerable is because the first time you experienced it, you were too young and vulnerable to know what to do with it. You felt it and you knew that you would die. Or that you are unlovable. Or that you are completely unsafe. This feeling is sitting on a mountain of the same old. So take this feeling that you have right now and time travel, using the feeling as the vehicle to transport you to the time when you first felt this way.

Step Three – Love Who You Were

You are an adult now. You have the capacity to give that little one all the love and assurance you needed as a small kid with a big booboo in your heart. Pour compassion, love, understanding and forgiveness into that little child.

Back in the day when that feeling was initially there, you didn't have the help to process it in a healthy way.

A part of you stayed stuck in there. Go back now and redeem yourself. Love yourself. Give that child the understanding and love to move forward, healed and whole.

This feeling is hard. If it's hard now, can you imagine how hard it was then? Give yourself as much compassion as you need.

Step Four – Analyze the Outcome

During that early time, the pain caused your little one to make certain decisions and take certain actions. Those decisions were based on pain, coupled with the limitations of the circumstances. This was a helpless little youngster who made decisions that still rule your life.

Let's look at that. What decisions did you make then? Did you decide to be less of who you were? Did you decide to hide who you really were, and to pretend to be who you were expected to be? To take care of others instead of yourself? To have no needs? Did you decide that things were your fault, and that you are a horrible person?

Those were decisions you made from a place of helplessness. But you are not helpless now. You are here to give yourself back to yourself. You are operating from a place of love. Seeing those decisions from your perspective today, even if you still believe that stuff, gives you back your own power.

Step Five – Love Who You Are

Now that you know better, give yourself permission to live from love. You can assure yourself whenever you feel lousy about yourself that it's okay to feel non-awesome. We all move through a variety of emotions, some that feel better than others. That's okay. Now you are in touch with your higher self, the self that is not bound by the pain-based decisions you made in a moment of utter helplessness. You are you, and you are love.

So while you walk through pain, remember your greatness. Say to yourself: I am love.

Chapter 8

Codependency: When Boundaries Disappear

Codependency is excessive emotional or psychological reliance on a partner, typically one who requires support. We enable another person's poor behavior by relying on that person for approval or a sense of identity.

Codependency is when taking care of others is more important than being happy yourself. You seek to find approval and worthiness in others.

Isn't it interesting that by relying on someone else, you are also enabling that individual to rely on you? When you create a dynamic where you need the other person to provide your sense of self, he needs you in turn, and is not okay without you. What a burden this becomes.

Naturally, this causes a problem with setting boundaries. What if that person becomes displeased? What if he gets angry? What if he abandons you?

When you have a hard time seeing your own worth, you can't know that you are worthy of respect. You continue to take abuse and blame yourself for it. You continue to overshare and overcompensate in the relationship, while the other person gives you little in return. You spend and expend yourself in the hope of redeeming your unworthiness.

The solution is to love yourself, as hard as it is, as undeserving as you think you are. Give yourself love. Begin to see yourself from a different perspective, one in which you let yourself off the hook. You see how powerful you are, and you courageously believe in your strengths. You create a dynamic of autonomy where you take care of yourself, and he, too, gets to ke a look at what you want

n. You share your message,

erson thinks.

:lationship

:rience

you, and you realize you

daries, your initial reaction

) it. That's good, but before

; the story back to yourself.

iurting you? This is about

you, so take your power back from the other person, back to yourself.

At times like this, we often feel confused or disempowered. We ask others for validation that what we are experiencing is indeed wrong. We ask for help in finding the right words. And while all of these are good steps to take, what you are really trying to do is find yourself inside of the situation. You're trying to validate and love yourself.

That's where you need to start. If the situation feels horrible, it's probably because it is. Validate that. Give compassion to your own self. Pause and be with yourself.

Step Two – Take Care of Yourself

Ask yourself: How can I love myself in this situation? What do I need? If I were a loving person in my own life, how would I care for myself?

And then go do that. If you are experiencing pain in a relationship, you want to heal yourself with love. Give yourself massive doses. What can I, me, do about this to take care of me? That's your focus. And whatever the answer is – "I need compassion, space, love, forgiveness" – listen to yourself and give it to yourself.

Your answer may be, "I need to get even, see the other person suffer, and tell it to her in a way that will finally make her go home and cry." Recognize that those feelings are valid, but also recognize that this boundary is external. You are still giving away your power to that other person.

Bring it back to you. That's where your healing lies.

Step Three - Communicate

When you are ready to take it to the other person – because you will have needs that must be met – ask yourself, "How can I communicate my needs for the sake of communicating my needs, and avoid communicating my needs for the sake of making them see?"

It is entirely possible that they can't see. But you are not in thier hands. You are not at thier disposal. You have the ability to advocate for you. You have your own back.

Clarify what it is that you want to communicate. It can be helpful to zoom out from the situation. You may have a specific need that needs to be met, but in a broader sense, what are you trying to create? What experience do you want? How do you want to go through your life?

When you say, "How dare you treat me this way," you are also saying, "I believe that I have a life waiting for me in which I am not backstabbed, not betrayed, not shamed." And what you are *really* saying is, "I know that I deserve to be treated respectfully, in real friendship, seen as an equal, and shining at life."

So say *that*. Be clear about that.

When you recognize that you are in a situation where you need to strengthen your boundaries, bring it back home and ask yourself about the pain that you're feeling, the internal push that tells you a line has been crossed. What is it saying about what your life should really be like?

That's your boundary. You. You knowing what you want in life. Once you know that, nobody can take that away. People may attempt to, but once you've seen yourself and your worth, you can't unsee it.

Conclusion

I wrote this book as a gift.

I didn't come into adulthood with boundaries. In fact, I allowed (maybe even invited) the most important people in my life to walk all over me with muddy shoes and stilettos. It was painful.

What followed were years of utter powerlessness. Until it got to be too much, and I decided to be brave enough to do the work of respecting myself. It wasn't easy work. It was courageous. I lost some friends. I lost my youth. But I gained myself, and I think that's the most valuable gift of all.

I know I'm not alone in this.

I've written this book for you if you don't love yourself. Or you do, but you're living with someone who doesn't act lovingly. You're discontent because you are not living the best life you can.

I want you to have yourself. You are the only one in the world who matters most. You have been charged with the one life that's been given to you. You must live a life in which you love yourself, and you love your days.

People may want to cross your boundaries. That's because they are them, it's not because you are you. What you have, and always will have, is the ability to calibrate and come back home to self. Your self is Your self is love. It's joy and it's yours.

given you as much as I could in one book. I set ach you how the boundary is really you, being ot about throwing everyone away, but about your priority and looking out for yourself, u would safeguard a precious object. Because at you are.

I want you to have all that you can. I want you to heal. I want you to feel love, and joy, and freedom. If I can be of service to you, please do not hesitate to reach out. My website www.chanyrosengarten.com has additional resources, including a full eight week course, as well as the ability to reach me, should you want my personal guidance.

I love you. I know you love you, too. I know that as you get in touch with that love more and more, you will learn to let others love you. And you will correct them if their love is misplaced. You will teach them how you like to be treated. I trust you on this one.

And with that, thank you for being brave enough for showing up for this book. That was self-love right there.

Much love,

Chany G. Rosengarten

About the author:

Chany G. Rosengarten is a wife, mother of four young children, bestselling author and powerful motivational speaker. She teaches empowerment, self-care and boundaries in business, love and relationships, and her online courses have changed the trajectory of many lives. To book a call with Chany, sign up here: https://calendly.com/chanybgcgr/book-a-call